The Gobi Desert

By Molly Aloian

🌳 Crabtree Publishing Company

www.crabtreebooks.com

Crabtree Publishing Company

www.crabtreebooks.com

Dedicated by Molly Aloian
For Andrew Urlocker—My oasis in the desert

Author: Molly Aloian
Publishing plan research and development:
Sean Charlebois, Reagan Miller
Crabtree Publishing Company
Editor: Adrianna Morganelli
Proofreader: Wendy Scavuzzo
Indexer: Wendy Scavuzzo
Graphic design and photo research:
Katherine Berti
Project coordinator: Kathy Middleton
Print and production coordinator:
Katherine Berti
Prepress technician: Margaret Salter

Front cover:
A hill rises from the Gobi Desert against
a brilliant sunrise.
Title page:
The desert surface in the Gobi Desert is
mostly bare rock and gravel.

Picture credits:
Shutterstock: chiakto: page 19; vincent369: page 25 (top);
pages 1, 4, 6 (top right), 7 (middle right and top right),
8, 10 (bottom), 12, 13, 14, 15 (top), 16 (top right), 18,
21, 24, 27, 28 (all bottom), front cover
Thinkstock: pages 5, 7 (left), 11 (both), 15 (bottom), 18,
20, 28 (top)
Dreamstime: pages 9 (bottom), 26 (both)
Wikimedia Commons: NASA MODIS Rapid Response
Team: page 6 (bottom right); Shizhao: pages 16
(bottom left), 25 (bottom); Inconnu, Atlas catalan:
page 17; Matt Affolter: page 21 (top); Library of
Congress: page 23
Canstock: page 22

Library and Archives Canada Cataloguing in Publication

CIP available at Library and Archives Canada

Library of Congress Cataloging-in-Publication Data

Aloian, Molly.
 The Gobi Desert / Molly Aloian.
   pages ; cm. -- (Deserts around the world)
 Includes index.
 ISBN 978-0-7787-0710-3 (reinforced library binding : alkaline paper)
 -- ISBN 978-0-7787-0718-9 (paperbadk : alkaline paper) -- ISBN
 (invalid) 978-1-4271-9045-1 (electronic pdf) -- ISBN (invalid) 978-1-
 4271-9099-4 (electronic html)
 1. Gobi Desert (Mongolia and China)--Juvenile literature. I. Title.
 II. Series: Deserts around the world (Crabtree Publishing Company)

 DS793.G6A46 2013
 951.7'3--dc23
                                  2012029159

Crabtree Publishing Company

www.crabtreebooks.com   1-800-387-7650
Printed in Hong Kong/ 092012/BK20120629

Published in Canada
Crabtree Publishing
616 Welland Ave.
St. Catharines, Ontario
L2M 5V6

Published in the United States
Crabtree Publishing
PMB 59051
350 Fifth Avenue, 59th Floor
New York, New York 10118

Published in the United Kingdom
Crabtree Publishing
Maritime House
Basin Road North, Hove
BN41 1WR

Published in Australia
Crabtree Publishing
3 Charles Street
Coburg North
VIC 3058

CONTENTS

Words that are defined in the glossary are in **bold** type the first time they appear in the text.

CHAPTER 1
The Great Gobi Desert

The Gobi Desert is a large desert in Asia. It covers about 500,000 square miles (1,294,994 sq km), stretching from the Tien Shan Mountains in the west and across southeastern Mongolia and northern China. The lack of rainfall in this huge area is the result of the **rain shadow** effect of the Himalayan mountains and the high **altitude** of the Tibetan **Plateau** to the south. The desert surface is mostly bare rock and gravel, but there are sand dunes in some places.

Unlike other deserts, the Gobi Desert contains few sand dunes. Instead, there are massive, barren rocky areas and large gravel plains.

FAST FACT
In Mongolian, the word "gobi" means "waterless place."

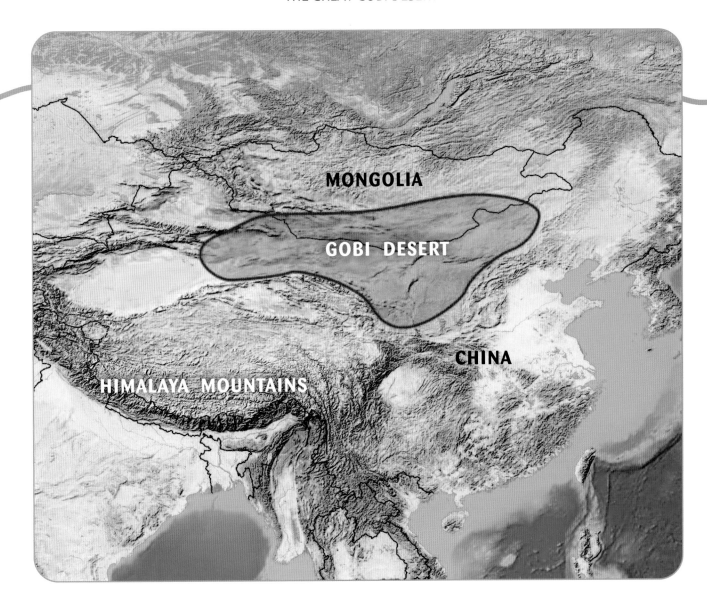

Parched Land

The Gobi Desert is extremely dry. Total precipitation per year varies from less than 2 inches (5 cm) in the west to more than 8 inches (20 cm) in the northeast. Winters in the Gobi are extremely severe. Average January temperatures are –40˚F (–40˚C). Spring is dry and cold, and summers are generally warm. In July, the average high is 113˚F (45˚C) in some areas.

Able to Survive

Despite the dry climate, grass, thornbushes, and other shrubs manage to grow. On the plateau and on the plains beneath the mountains, plants such as yellowwood bean caper, winterfat, and nitre bush, can be found. Mammals, including Bactrian camels, jerboas, gophers, and black-tailed gazelle, as well birds, amphibians, and various reptiles also call the desert home. These plants and animals have **adapted** to the harsh desert conditions and are able to survive with little to no water.

Human Inhabitants

The Gobi's severe, rocky, and dry landscape and its harsh summer and winter weather have prevented extensive human settlement, but humans have lived in the Gobi for thousands of years. In fact, fragments of 100,000-year-old stone weapons and tools have been found in the Gobi's soils. These items belonged to **nomads** who hunted and gathered throughout the desert. The desert was also part of the Silk Road, which was a 4,000-mile (6,437-km) network of trade routes that connected Europe and Asia for 3,000 years. Today, the desert is sparsely populated. There are Mongols and Han Chinese people, but there are fewer than three people per square mile (2.6 sq km). Scientists and tourists travel through the Gobi Desert to explore the dramatic landscape and to visit the nomadic peoples who are still living in their traditional ways.

In the Gobi, people can travel almost anywhere by camel. Riding camels is a popular form of transportation.

Desert in Danger

Since the 1980s, **industrialization** has caused environmental pollution in the desert. For example, the manufacturing of chemical fertilizers in the Hohhot area has **contaminated** groundwater. Thousands of people have also been affected by contaminated well water. Today, the Gobi Desert is expanding at an alarming rate in a process called **desertification**. This has caused an increased number of dust storms, which is damaging China's agricultural economy.

A dust storm occurs where soil is extremely dry and has few plants to hold the soil in place. Strong winds blow across the surface of the area, carrying the dusty soil away with it. After very violent dust storms, it is sometimes impossible to grow crops again for many years.

Hot or Cold

Most deserts are very hot places, but not all deserts are hot. Some deserts can get quite cold during the year. Some are even covered with ice or snow. There is little precipitation in these deserts, but the temperature is so cold the snow does not melt. The Gobi Desert is often considered a cold desert. This is due to its northern location and its high altitude. Parts of the Gobi are thousands of feet above sea level.

Some areas of the Gobi Desert contain large numbers of dinosaur bones. **Fossils** of dinosaurs, such as the four-legged beaked Protoceratops, have been found **eroding** out of the desert hillsides for thousands of years.

Snow leopards once roamed across the Gobi Desert in great numbers, but the population has dwindled as the human population has grown. As the human population grows, these big cats are pushed out of the grasslands and pastures of the Tibetan Plateau and the high mountain valleys of Xinjiang. Experts estimate that there are only about 4,000–6,000 snow leopards left on Earth.

Trained to Keep Track

In 2004, 27-year-old environmentalist Jargal Jamsranjav won The Whitley Award for International Nature Conservation. She spent time training Mongolian herders in scientific research skills so they could help monitor the dwindling wildlife populations in the Gobi and other regions. She has also helped Mongolian people adopt important conservation methods, such as avoiding **overgrazing**, conserving water, and managing waste more effectively.

CHAPTER 2

Dry Times

A desert can be defined in different ways, but many scientists believe that a desert is an area that receives less than 10 inches (25 cm) of rain per year. Deserts lose more moisture through evaporation than they receive from precipitation. They may seem to be barren wastelands, but deserts contain a vast array of plants and animals that have adapted to the harsh conditions.

Today, there are less than 1,000 Bactrian camels left on Earth. They are **endangered** animals.

Desert Design

Bactrian camels have bodies that are designed for life in the brutal Gobi Desert. They have two humps rather than one. The humps store fat, which can be converted into water and energy when food and water is not available. The humps allow the camels to endure long periods of travel without water, even in the hottest, driest conditions. Bactrian camels also have thick, shaggy coats that help keep them warm in winter. As the seasons change and temperatures become warmer, they shed their heavy coats. Bactrian camels rarely sweat, which also helps them conserve fluids for long periods of time. They have long eyelashes and nostrils that close to keep out sand. Wide footpads help the camels walk over rough, rocky terrain and shifting desert sands without sinking under their own weight.

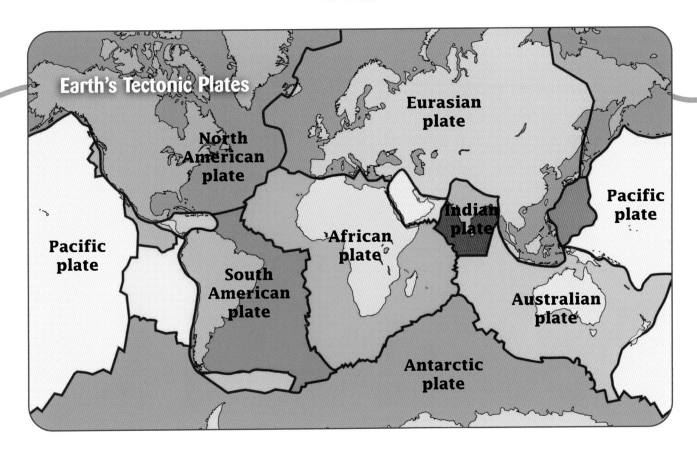

Earth's Tectonic Plates

North American plate

Eurasian plate

Pacific plate

Pacific plate

African plate

Indian plate

South American plate

Australian plate

Antarctic plate

High and Dry

According to **geologists**, the Gobi Desert began to form millions of years ago. About 50 million years ago, during the period of Earth's history called the Eocene epoch, two of Earth's **tectonic plates** crashed together. The Indian Plate crashed into the Eurasian Plate. The sheer force of this crash caused massive uplifting and twisting. It caused the entire Tibetan Plateau to raise more than 16,000 feet (4,877 m) above sea level. The Gobi occupies part of this plateau, about 3,000 feet (914 m) above sea level in the east and 5,000 feet (1,524 m) in the west. The high **atmospheric pressure** in this region can cause dry, cold air from the upper altitudes to compress and come down to Earth. The sun heats this dry air, causing high temperatures and low humidity.

The peaks of the Qilian Mountain Range rise from about 18,000 feet (5,486 m) to more than 20,000 feet (6,096 m).

Rain Shadow

Another factor in the formation of the Gobi is the Himalayan mountains. The Indian Plate and the Eurasian Plate both had the same rock densities when they crashed millions of years ago, so one plate could not be pushed under the other. The colliding plates thrust upward and folded, bended, and twisted against one another. This formed the jagged, immense peaks of the Himalayas. The Gobi Desert is locked deep inside the landmass between the mountains. The desert is in a **rain shadow**. A rain shadow is a dry area of land on the leeward side of a mountainous area. Rainfall and moist air prevail on the windward side of the Himalayas, while arid moisture-poor air prevails on the leeward side of the mountains. This means that any moist air loses most of its precipitation before reaching the Gobi. The Gobi is also very far away from an ocean, which is the primary source of moisture for rainfall.

FAST FACT

Although the size of Earth's deserts is always changing, deserts cover from 5–7 percent of Earth's surface. The Atacama Desert in Chile is the driest place on Earth. Each year, it receives less than 0.01 inches (0.03 cm) of rain.

The Himalayas, stretching for more than 1,500 miles (2,414 km) from east to west across Asia, played an important role in the formation of the Gobi Desert. The desert formed because the Himalayas blocked rain-carrying clouds from reaching the region.

Five Regions

Some scientists divide the Gobi Desert into five distinct ecological regions. There are different plants and animals living in each of these regions. Every plant and animal is adapted to the dry climate. The five regions are the eastern Gobi desert **steppe**, the Alashan Plateau, the Gobi Lakes Valley, the Junggar **Basin** (Dzungarian Basin), and the Tian Shan range. The eastern Gobi desert steppe contains drought-resistant shrubs and scattered low grasses, as well as a number of mammals and birds. The Alashan Plateau is the largest of the Gobi's eco-regions and contains the Great Gobi National Park.

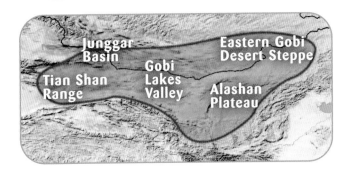

The Gobi Lakes Valley has a few sand dunes interspersed with salt marshes and other wetlands that are home to water birds, amphibians, and various reptiles. The Junggar Basin contains shrubs and woodlands and some of the rarest animals on Earth. The Tian Shan range contains a number of rare animal species, as well as shrubs, grasses, and poplar trees.

Rivers flowing from the Kangai Mountains feed the salt marshes in the Gobi Lakes Valley. During droughts, however, the rivers do not always carry enough water down the mountains.

Threats to the Desert

Unfortunately, all of the Gobi's eco-regions have been affected negatively by the actions of humans. Overgrazing, **irrigation** agriculture, overhunting, and mining are some of the factors that are threatening the overall health of the desert and the unique plants and animals that live there.

Awesome Adaptations

Many Gobi Desert plants have long roots that can absorb water from a large area. Winterfat is a shrub that is covered in densely matted hairs. The hairs help protect the plant from the hot and cold temperatures. They also prevent the plant from losing moisture through evaporation. The saxaul is a bush-like tree that grows throughout the Gobi. Its bark holds moisture for the plant. Its small leaves also help to minimize the loss of moisture.

The saxaul ranges in size from a large shrub to a small tree from 6.5 to 26 feet (2 to 8 m) tall. Its wood is heavy and the bark is spongy and waterlogged.

Saxaul Saves the Day

The saxaul is one of the most important and useful native plants in the region from the Caspian Sea eastward across the Gobi Desert. Over time, this plant has adapted to the dry, windy, and **saline** conditions in this arid region. It has become an important natural resource for the people of the Gobi Desert because it is sometimes the only plant growing in harsh habitats such as sand, dry canyons, and rocky hill and mountain slopes.

People press its moisture-rich bark to extract precious drinking water. Its wood provides fuel for campfires for heat and cooking. The wild Bactrian camel, the ibex, and various bird species also rely on the saxaul for food and shelter. Traditional weavers from Turkmenistan use a green dye from the plant's wood to color yarn. This yarn is then woven into their **exquisite** carpets. The plant also helps prevent erosion from wind and slows down the process of desertification.

There are rivers in the Gobi, but most only flow in the summer when the desert receives its small amount of rainfall. Rivers that flow into the region from the surrounding mountains quickly disappear into the dry ground.

NOTABLE QUOTE

"The driest places on Earth, deserts are home to 350 million people and some of the rarest and most curious species of plants and animals known."

—Achim Steiner, Executive Director of the United Nations Environment Programme (UNEP)

CHAPTER 3

Living in the Gobi

People have been living in the Gobi Desert for thousands of years. Many of the people living in the desert today still live in traditional ways. The desert provides them with enough food and water to raise cattle and other animals and sustain a nomadic or semi-nomadic way of life. Early peoples in the Gobi Desert were mainly nomads, as well. By the 13th century, Italian explorer Marco Polo was one of the only Europeans to have traveled through the desert.

This picture shows Jiayuguan, which was built during the early Ming dynasty. It was the first pass on the west end of the Great Wall of China.

FAST FACT

In the Mongolian language, there are 33 different words for *desert*.

Ancient Peoples

The Gobi Desert appears empty and barren, but there have always been people living in it. Ancient Mongolian peoples hunted and gathered throughout the desert for thousands of years. They were nomadic traders and herdsmen. They traveled in groups and raised goats, cattle, camels, horses, and sheep. The animals provided people with meat, milk, transportation, and wool. These ancient peoples traded with peoples around them for grain, rice, tea, silk, and other items.

The traditional dwellings of Mongolian peoples were called *gers* or *yurts*. They were circular structures made from wooden poles and covered with animal skins, woven cloth, or felt.

The Mongolian Gobi

In the 12th century, the Gobi became part of the Mongol Empire—the biggest land empire in history. Its territory extended from the Yellow Sea in eastern Asia to the borders of eastern Europe. At different times, the Mongol Empire included China, Korea, Mongolia, Persia (now present-day Iran), Turkestan, and Armenia. When Genghis Khan decided to overtake China, he and his warriors crossed the Gobi Desert. They followed special trails and drove herds of cattle through the desert, which provided them with meat and milk.

Silk Road

In the 13th century, the southern edge of the Gobi Desert was part of the Silk Road, a 4,000-mile (6,437-km) long network of trade routes that connected eastern, southern, and western Asia with parts of the Mediterranean and Europe, as well as parts of northern and eastern Africa. The Silk Road was used to transport silk and spices from Asia, and gold, silver, precious stones, and cloth from Europe. Other luxury trade goods included medicines, perfume, and glassware.

Genghis Khan founded the Mongol Empire, which became the largest empire in history following his death in 1227.

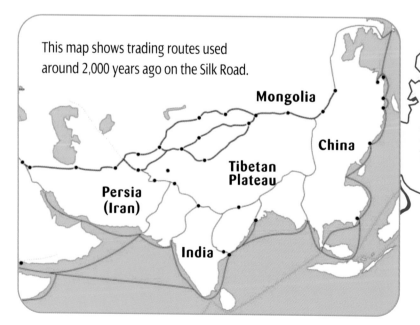

This map shows trading routes used around 2,000 years ago on the Silk Road.

Mongolia

China

Tibetan Plateau

Persia (Iran)

India

FAST FACT

When the first Chinese silk cloth reached Europe, it was literally worth its weight in gold. No one knew how to make it because Chinese silk-makers were extremely secretive about their methods.

On the Move

The people living in desert communities along the Silk Road witnessed these special goods moving through the desert.

In the 13th century, the Italian explorer and merchant Marco Polo visited some of these Silk Road communities as he crossed the Gobi Desert. Marco Polo crossed the Gobi with a caravan, which is a group of people traveling together. The caravan encountered many dangers while crossing the Gobi, but Polo's account of the expedition suggests that the route was safe and very well established.

Crossing the Gobi

Marco Polo (1254–1324) was a merchant traveler from Venice, Italy. He was one of the first Europeans to travel across Asia through China, and one of the first Europeans to set foot in the Gobi. In 1271, he embarked on an epic 24-year journey to Asia with his father and uncle. They sailed south from Venice, Italy, across the Mediterranean Sea to the Middle East. They then headed southeast on land to Persia (present-day Iran), through the Pamir Mountains and the Gobi Desert to Beijing, China. They also explored the area south of Beijing before traveling east to the Yangtze River and south to Hangchow, China. They then sailed south to present-day Vietnam and Sumatra, and west to Sri Lanka and India.

This drawing shows some of the men in Marco Polo's caravan crossing the Gobi Desert.

NOTABLE QUOTE

"This desert is reported to be so long that it would take a year to go from end to end; and at the narrowest point it takes a month to cross it. It consists entirely of mountains and sands and valleys. There is nothing at all to eat."

—Marco Polo, 13th century explorer

Desert Dwellers

Today, the people of the Gobi Desert are mainly Khalkha Mongols. Khalkha Mongols are semi-nomadic and usually live in family groups. For their survival, they depend on herds of Bactrian camels, which have been used in the region for thousands of years. They use the camels for transportation, and many herdsmen keep sheep and goats for meat and yarn. Khalkha people move to new areas about 10 times each year. Some moves are short to reach fresh pastureland for animals. Other moves are longer seasonal moves to escape the coldest, hottest, or driest weather. At the edges of the Gobi, in the Inner Mongolian Autonomous Region of the Peoples Republic of China, Chinese people make up the majority of the population. The Chinese people are mainly farmers who grow food crops, but the growing season is extremely short. They live in small homes built out of clay bricks.

The *Ger*

Living in lightweight *gers* makes moving from place to place easier for people living in the Gobi Desert. The *ger* has a wooden framework and is covered with layers of animal hides and woven fabric, which are tied into place. It provides warmth in the bitterly cold winter and remains cool in the scorching summer temperatures. It is a light and strong shelter that is easy to assemble, take apart, move, and then reassemble. The inside of the *ger* is usually simply furnished. Some contain brightly colored rugs decorated with geometric or stylized animal patterns.

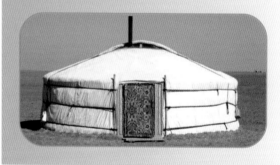

Endangered Gobi Bear

The Gobi bear, known in Mongolia as Mazaalai, is a **critically endangered** bear living in Mongolia. Today, scientists estimate that there may be as few as 20–25 bears remaining in the wild. They live in the Great Gobi Strictly Protected Area. In 2004, a workshop was held to develop a plan to help save the Gobi bear. A total of 75 participants were involved in the workshop, including 10 international experts, Ministry of Nature and Environment personnel, park staff, local environmental specialists, and non-governmental organizations. Participants were urged to develop specific recommendations to help conserve the Gobi bear.

A nomadic woman milks her goats. Goats are a major source of meat and milk for those living in the Gobi Desert.

NOTABLE QUOTE

"Most of these people have never seen a mobile phone, never seen a computer. Nomgom is their only link to the developed world – providing school, hospital, post office and – for a few hours a day – electricity. In other parts of Mongolia, which have been hit by very bad winters and drought, people have had to move to the city to survive. But the people here don't want to do that."

—Jargal Jamsranjav, environmentalist

CHAPTER 4
Travel and Commerce

People have been traveling through the Gobi Desert since ancient times. They trekked over the treacherous terrain to locate pastureland for their animals, and to trade new and valuable goods with people from other parts of the world. Today, people are still traveling through the Gobi, and its natural resources help support the region's economy.

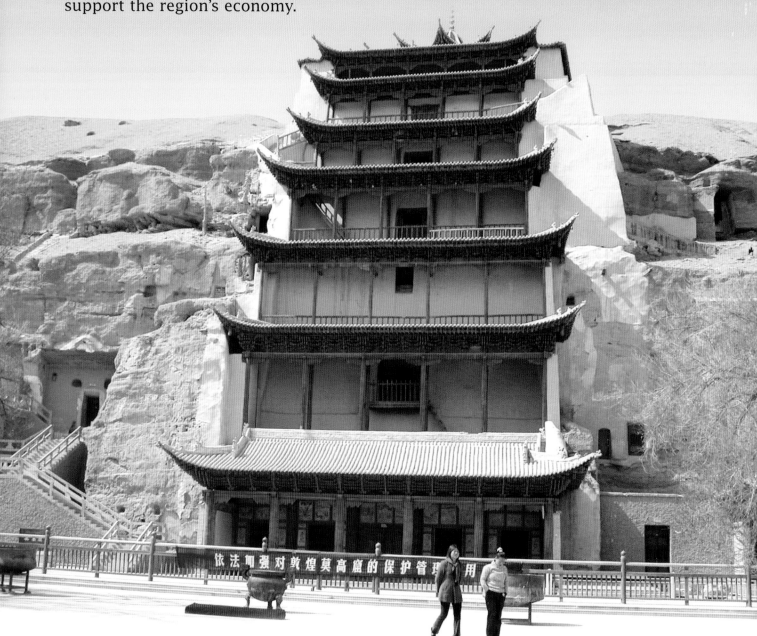

A series of Buddhist cave-temples, called the Mogao Caves, near the city of Dunhuang in Gansu province, China, are a very popular tourist destination in the Gobi. The caves are famous for their statues and wall paintings. In 1987, the caves were declared a UNESCO World Heritage Site.

More Water!

In ancient times, there were a number of **oases** in the Gobi. These places provided rest stops for people traveling in caravans. Unfortunately, these settlements only flourished until their populations became too great for their water supply. Today, the main factor preventing human expansion in the Gobi is still the lack of water.

A flash flood in the Gobi Desert can occur very suddenly and with little warning. This type of flood can be very dangerous.

Changing Lifestyle

At present, there are a few small towns in the Gobi, such as those along the Beijing-Ulaanbaatar railroad. Motorized vehicles are slowly becoming more common, but have not yet replaced the traditional forms of transportation. There are also administration centers, which provide special services for nomadic and semi-nomadic peoples raising herds of animals. For example, there is a boarding school system for the children of the herdspeople. The school provides the children with daily education that is not disrupted by the nomadic lifestyle of their parents.

Erdene Zuu Monastery is one of the oldest Buddhist monasteries in Mongolia.

Discovering Oil

Oil was discovered in the Gobi near the town of Saynshand in the northeastern part of the region. Chinese people started using the oil, and miners began digging deeper into the ground to find more. However, the fact that the area has little water to sustain large populations, as well as being extremely remote, meant that oil production would contribute very little to the region's economy.

Yours and Mine

Other natural resources in the Gobi include salt, coal, petroleum, copper, and other ores. Today, international mining corporations are digging into the ground for coal, copper, and gold to send to China. The mines are expected to help Mongolia's economy grow by more than 20 percent per year for the next two decades. China accounts for 85 percent of Mongolia's exports, so the people of Mongolia are hoping these mega-mines will bring in more money. Many people fear the worst, however.

Hit the Ground

The Xinjiang ground jay is another threatened species that lives in the Gobi Desert. As its name suggests, it lives only in Xinjiang in Western China where it is found in sandy desert areas and in the scrub of the Taklimakan Desert. The ground jay population is declining because of habitat loss from the overgrazing of goats and camels. Huge areas of its habitat are also being converted into irrigated land.

NOTABLE QUOTE

"How much can an ecosystem take until it collapses? We don't know enough yet about the Gobi to answer... At the moment it is all piecemeal, mine by mine, project by project. If they carry on down that road, there will be a lot of problems ahead."

—Kirk Olsen, wildlife expert

Tourism

Many people visit the Gobi Desert to view the spectacular landscapes and rare wildlife, and to better understand its unique ecosystems. Some travel to the desert to visit parts of the Silk Road. **Paleontologists** and archaeologists in search of buried bones and other remnants from ancient cultures are also drawn to the Gobi Desert.

Some people suggest that Roy Chapman Andrews was the inspiration for the fictional adventurer/ **archaeologist** Indiana Jones from George Lucas's movie franchise of the same name.

Dinosaur Expedition

In the 1920s and 1930s, a caravan of scientists from the American Museum of Natural History in New York City bravely journeyed into the heart of the Mongolian Gobi Desert on five expeditions. They were searching for fossils. They endured violent dust storms, drought, exhaustion, and other hardships, but returned home with an abundance of mammal and dinosaur fossils including dinosaur eggs. A man named Roy Chapman Andrews led the scientists on the expedition. Andrews later wrote an autobiography called *Under a Lucky Star* about his time in the Gobi.

RacingThePlanet

In 2002, marathon runner Mary K. Gadams founded a company called RacingThePlanet. The company was one of the first to set up off-trail or rough-country endurance footraces. Today, the company organizes several endurance races, one of which is the 4 Deserts Race. People from all over the world compete in seven-day 155-mile (250-km) footraces through the world's deserts. Participants can race through the Atacama Desert in Chile, the Gobi Desert in China, the Sahara in Egypt, and the icy desert in Antarctica. They can tackle all of the desert races, or just one if they choose. The first race across the Gobi Desert, called the Gobi March, took place in September 2003. There were 42 competitors facing the challenges of the Gobi—the changes in temperature from the cool highlands to the sweltering heat in sand dunes, the total lack of shade, potential sandstorms, and a variety of difficult terrain including steep hills, rocky paths, soft sand dunes, ridges, and riverbeds. In 2012, RacingThePlanet celebrated its 10th anniversary. The 2012 Gobi March took place around the region of Kashgar.

CHAPTER 5

Great Gobi at Risk

The Gobi Desert may appear to be harsh and unforgiving to the plants, animals, and people that live there, but the desert is actually extremely fragile. The unique plants and animals in the desert are constantly under threat from irrigation agriculture, industry, overgrazing, mining, and other activities. Environmental organizations are starting to realize the need to protect the Gobi Desert and the plants, animals, and people living within it.

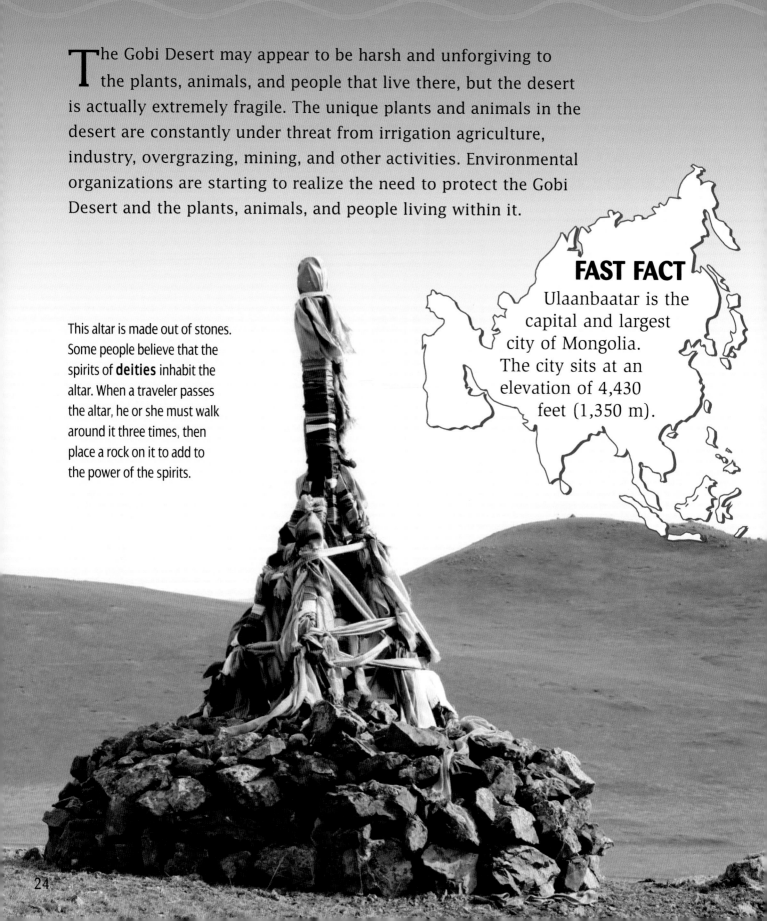

This altar is made out of stones. Some people believe that the spirits of **deities** inhabit the altar. When a traveler passes the altar, he or she must walk around it three times, then place a rock on it to add to the power of the spirits.

FAST FACT
Ulaanbaatar is the capital and largest city of Mongolia. The city sits at an elevation of 4,430 feet (1,350 m).

A serious sandstorm rages through the city of Beijing on March 20, 2010.

Growth of the Desert

Desertification is a major problem in the Gobi Desert and around the world. Since 1994, the Gobi Desert in China has expanded by about 25,000 square miles (64,750 sq km) and its sands are slowly encroaching on the capital city of Beijing. China is among the countries worst affected by desertification. Beijing gets blasted by over half a million tons of sand every year. Air traffic stops, people are forced to stay indoors, and highways are inundated with sand. The Chinese government has spent millions of dollars trying to stop desertification, but it cannot seem to keep up with the rapid expansion of the desert.

Sandstorms in Beijing usually occur in spring because it is still windy and dry. Beijing officials issue pollution warnings throughout the city and warn people to stay indoors.

Less Land

Large areas of the Gobi are being taken up by people trying to raise food crops and using up what little water is available. When land is used for irrigated agriculture, there is less land available for livestock grazing. Furthermore, irrigated agricultural areas are most often set up on the land that is most needed for livestock grazing—the wet pastures near rivers. Nomadic and semi-nomadic peoples rely on livestock for their survival, so this lack of water and pasture for grazing poses a serious threat to the human population.

There are farms of food crops in some of the more hospitable parts of the Gobi Desert.

Minding Mines

Mines in the Gobi present a massive environmental challenge. Roads and trucks leading to and from the mines disrupt the nomadic and semi-nomadic communities living in the Gobi. Operating the mines requires vast quantities of precious water per day and has negative impacts on the nomadic and semi-nomadic peoples living throughout the area. They blame the mines for dried-up wells, shrinking watering holes, and clouds of dust that blacken their lungs and the lungs of their animals.

This copper mine in Xinjiang, China, is one of many mines that depletes the precious water supply in the Gobi Dessert.

The Saxaul Suffers

The saxaul is slowly disappearing from the Gobi Desert. Over the past several decades, forests of this precious natural resource have shrunk dramatically in many areas. Some experts believe it is suffering as a result of **climate change**, which may be further increasing the Gobi's already arid conditions. Part of the saxaul's decline is also due to the growth of the human population in the desert. More and more people are relying on the plant's wood for fuel instead of the expensive coal and petroleum-based products that are being mined by wealthy, multinational corporations.

Conserve and Protect

Governments and environmental organizations are working hard to conserve and protect the Gobi Desert and all the living things that rely on it for survival. Laws have been passed to protect desert species, and certain areas of the Gobi have been set aside as parks and nature reserves. For example, nature reserves have been established in China to protect the Bactrian camel: the Altun Mountain National Nature Reserve and the Lop Nur Wild Camel National Nature Reserve are both in Xinjiang. Scientists, environmental experts, and wildlife specialists are also taking the time to study and understand the delicate balance of life in the Gobi Desert. As scientists and environmentalists learn more about the desert, they will be better able to protect it for generations to come.

NOTABLE QUOTE

"The camels have literally been saved from extinction, but there is so much more to be done, so much more to help protect the environment…and to improve the lives of the Mongolians."

—Dr. Jane Goodall

COMPARING THE WORLD'S DESERTS

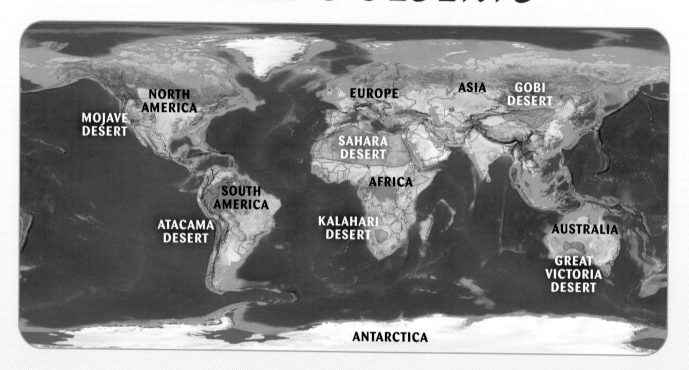

	Continent	Approximate Size	Type of Desert	Annual Precipitation	Natural Resources
Atacama	South America	140,000 square miles (362,598 sq km)	coastal desert	less than 4 inches (10 cm)	copper, sodium nitrate, salt, lithium
Gobi	Asia	500,000 square miles (1,294,994 sq km)	cold desert	2–8 inches (5–20 cm)	Oil, coal, copper, gold, petroleum, salt
Great Victoria	Australia	161,700 square miles (418,800 sq km)	hot, dry desert	8–10 inches (20–25 cm)	gold, opal, iron ore, copper, coal, oil
Kalahari	Africa	275,000 square miles (712,247 sq km)	semi-arid desert, arid savannah	5–25 inches (13–64 cm)	Coal, copper, nickel, and diamonds
Mojave	North America	25,000 square miles (64,750 sq km)	hot, dry desert	2–6 inches (5–15 cm)	Copper, gold, solar power
Sahara	Africa	3.5 million square miles (9.1 million sq km)	hot, dry desert	3–5 inches (8–13 cm)	Coal, oil, natural gas, various minerals

TIMELINE

Between 40 and 50 million years ago	Part of Earth's crust under India slams into the crust of Asia, forming the Tibetan Plateau and the Himalayas
Around 20,000 years ago	The ancient Uyghur (Uighur) Empire begins
2nd century B.C.E. to 14th century C.E.	The Silk Road extends for 4,000 miles (6,437 km), passing through parts of the Gobi Desert
1206–1227	Genghis Khan is leader of the Mongol Empire
1271–1295	Marco Polo travels from Europe to Asia, passing through the Gobi and keeping records of his trip
1585	Abtai Sain Khan builds the Erdene Zuu Monastery in Mongolia
1922–1925	Roy Chapman Andrews discovers dinosaur bones and dinosaur eggs in the Gobi Desert
1955	Oil is discovered in the Gobi Desert
1975	The Mongolian government establishes the Great Gobi Strictly Protected Area
1990	Scientists from the American Museum of Natural History are given the opportunity to develop an expedition to the Gobi Desert in search of fossils
1991	The United Nations designates the Gobi Desert as an International Biosphere Reserve, the largest reserve in Asia
2006	The year 2006 is declared the International Year of Deserts and Desertification
2008	Bactrian camels are listed as critically endangered on the IUCN's red list
2012	Vicente Garcia Beneito from Spain wins the Gobi March, earning his second-straight 4 Deserts victory

GLOSSARY

adapted Changed to fit a new or specific use or situation

altitude The vertical elevation of a region or area

archaeologists People who study past human life through fossils

atmospheric pressure The pressure in the surrounding air at or close to the surface of Earth

basin The land drained by a river and its tributaries

climate change A long-term, lasting change in the weather conditions in an area

contaminated Made impure or unfit for use by adding something harmful or unpleasant

critically endangered Describes animals that are at high risk of dying out in the wild

deities Beings with divine qualities or powers; gods or goddesses

desertification The gradual development of desert-like conditions

endangered Describes animals that are at risk of dying out in the world

eroding Wearing away

exquisite Describing something intricate and beautiful

fossils The remains of long-dead plants or animals that are preserved in earth or rock

geologists People who study the history of Earth and its life, especially as recorded in rocks

industrialization The process of social and economic change whereby a society changes from mainly agricultural to being mainly industrial

irrigation Supplying crops with water by artificial means

nomads People with no fixed home, who instead move from place to place

oases Fertile or green places in deserts

overgrazing Allowing animals to feed on grass or other plants to the point of destroying the vegetation

paleontologists Scientists that study the life of past geologic periods through fossil remains

plateau A flat area of high land

rain shadow An area of dry land on the leeward (or downwind) side of a mountain

saline Containing salt

steppe A vast area of land that is dry, flat, and covered with short grasses, shrubs, and trees

tectonic plates Giant pieces of Earth's crust

FIND OUT MORE

BOOKS

Facklam, Margery. *Tracking Dinosaurs in the Gobi*. Millbrook Press, 2004.

Hyde, Natalie. *Desert Extremes* (Extreme Nature). Crabtree Publishing Company, 2009.

Kalman, Bobbie. *China: the land* (Lands, Peoples, & Cultures). Crabtree Publishing Company, 2008.

Latham, Donna. *Deserts* (Endangered Biomes). Nomad Press, 2010.

Star, Fleur. *Desert* (Eye Wonder). DK Publishing, 2007.

Stille, Darlene R. *Deserts* (True Books: Earth Science). Children's Press, 2000.

WEBSITES

Gobi Desert
http://gobidesert.org/

Lop Nur Nature Reserve
www.wildcamels.com/what-we-do/lop-nur-nature-reserve/

WWF – Gobi Desert
http://wwf.panda.org/about_our_earth/teacher_resources/best_place_species/current_top_10/gobi_desert.cfm

Gobi Desert – National Geographic Education
http://education.nationalgeographic.com/education/multimedia/gobi-desert/?ar_a=2&ar_r=999

Global Greenhouse Warming – Gobi Desert
www.global-greenhouse-warming.com/gobi-desert.html

Gobi March (China) 2012 Official Website
www.4deserts.com/gobimarch/

Ancient China: The Silk Road
www.ducksters.com/history/china/silk_road.php

INDEX